Halfway Decent Sinners

Halfway Decent Sinners

Poems by Michael Cleary

CustomWords

© 2006 by Michael Cleary

Published by CustomWords
P.O. Box 541106
Cincinnati, OH 45254-1106

Typeset in Goudy Old Style by WordTech Communications LLC,
Cincinnati, OH

ISBN: 1933456191
LCCN: 2006922600

Poetry Editor: Kevin Walzer
Business Editor: Lori Jareo

Visit us on the web at www.custom-words.com

Acknowledgments

My gratitude to journals which published these poems, some in slightly different versions. *Berkeley Poetry Review:* "Ruminations on Free Will (with Pelicans)"; *The Cape Rock:* "In the Year I'm Old As My Father Ever Was"; *Cumberland Poetry Review:* "His Daughter Climbs a Florida Mountain," "Square Dancing with Sister Robert Claire," "Telling the Children," "Aunt Sara at the Yard Sale," "Original Sin"; *Freshwater:* "Sister Lard Ass and the Squirt Gun"; *Louisiana Literature:* "Paramount Theater: Solipsism in the '50s"; *The Litchfield Review:* "Second Marriage Polka"; *Pegasus:* "First Florida Summer," "Second Florida Summer"; *The Pegasus Review:* "Aunt Sara's February Dream"; *Poet Lore:* "Agnostic's Horoscope," "Lucky Shirt"; *Poetry Motel:* "Body English"; *Portland Review:* "Visiting Hours at the VA Hospital," "Blue Barns Road"; *Slant:* "Selfish Wants"; *Sport Literate:* "Boys Skinny-Dipping at the 'Y' in Winter"; *Talisman:* "Umbilicus in My Daughter's Diaper"; *The Texas Review:* "Dirty Jokes," "Boss's Son"; *To Honor a Teacher (Anthology):* "Square Dancing with Sister Robert Claire"; *Wind:* "Chemo Sabe."

Two Individual Artist Fellowships from the State of Florida assisted in completion of several poems.

Thanks to family and friends whose adventures, foibles, and great good humor offer something worth writing about.

For Carol—

Loveliness to grace my clumsy heart.

Contents

Original Sins

Lucky Shirt

fffffffffft. ffft. fffffffffffft.
The sound flutters in the air
like a question answered
by the miracle of a tiny bird
of a woman puffing into a tube
commands the wheelchair follows,
lungs stronger than legs
bent beneath her like broken wings.

The man flails on rubbery legs
buckling. Muscles and nerves and brain
discombobulating,
a sideshow I can't stop watching—
See *The Incredible Spastic Man!*
Hip bones forgetting thigh bones;
thigh bones forgetting knee bones.

An aide pushes the boy in a wheelchair.
His body thrust back-back like an astronaut,
chin angled fiercely up; eyes
exploring the ceiling like constellations.
Across his chest the words, Lucky Shirt.

Lucky Shirt. Meaning—what?
A curse? A joke? A prayer?
Such everyday unbearableness.

I want a shirt that says, *Sisyphus aint no sissy.*
Who knows what words will save us
or what grace we deserve in the end.
But what strength. What holy spirit
moves in mysterious human ways,
courage that blesses us as we praise.

Paramount Theater:
Solipsism in the '50s

We grew up on them, so names
of streets meant nothing to us
but neighborhoods—places
closer than history, more common than trees.
Washington. Lexington. Lincoln. Sherman. Grant.
Elm. Pine. Park. Walnut. Cherry. Grove.
Some were plain and simply
adjacent until we learned better in school.
Orville and Wilbur. Ft. Amherst and Garrison.
Mohican and Fenimore and Cooper.

On Food Drive Saturday mornings
our parents sent us down those streets
to the Paramount loaded with cans
of soup, baked beans, ravioli, stew.
Whoever the poor people were, they seemed
far from us as the mural ceiling
with its fabulous chariot race in the sky.
From the balcony we watched *The Robe*,
Demetrius and the Gladiators, Ben-Hur.
The dreary rote of Catechism turned
Technicolor and CinemaScope and Real.

One summer afternoon
Boom-Boom and I found the backstage door open
to fresh air and not a soul inside.
We never wondered what made us do it
or worried about what could happen.
Climbing up to the back row seats
we bolted forward, leaping on chair backs
like railroad ties all the way down,

then up again and down and out to the alley.
Never wondering what kept us from falling
or getting caught or why, with no tickets gone,
someone showed the movie on time
so beyond us other lives spoke to each other,
flickered, made their way in the dark.

Body English

That last second
wriggle-y   jiggle-y
herky-jerk-jerky
joke.

The body talking
to its self, saying only
I'm sorry. I'm sorry.
Please please please please please.

A sacrifice of dignity
on the altar of luck.
The least hope
of some easygoing god.

Confession

My wife, gentle and patient, swears
by the pup's breed: *all good; eager to please.*
I want to believe, still heartily sorry
for times before, following my father's way
while learning to detest it even more:
shouts to the beat of newspapers thwacking;
muzzles ground into awful mouthfuls.

But weeks of coming inside only
to mess moments later and twice
gnawing halfway through French doors
wear us down to compromise: a return
to crude necessity, but firmly resolved
to be twice as calm, half as rough.
So next time, I nudge her nose
to the puddle; stern words to memorize
the taste of *No. No. Bad Girl.*
Each time, her squirming harder
to restrain, her dread
a bellyful of thorns
I remember from confessionals:
God's wrath in dry whispers, just
punishments to help me sin no more.

As she complies, I offer praise and confirmation
—*Good Girl! Good Girl!*—
But the language of her body
doing its work defies such lies:
eyes white with sidelong glances;
shoulders slumped as if condemned;
back arched to bear the weight of

Bad and *No* all her days,
the price we learn to pay
for soiling a God-given world.

Learning Picasso

Painting is a mediator between this strange
hostile world and us… giving form to our terrors
as well as our desires.

                              –Pablo Picasso

Warren Street: a peeling three story monstrosity
with porches and bulging balconies
we covered with watered down Tawny Gold.
Across the street: The Hyde Collection's stately elegance.
Inside, highbrows and high mucketymucks
the snide world over had Rembrandt, Renoir
and who-knows-who all at their call.
Slapdash painting was all we numbskulls knew.
Consider the landlord's daily joke:
"Move yer ass, Michelangelo, it aint no church!"
The very top of the turret
we put off til last day, its six-foot spire
the high point of a lowdown summer job—
then discovered our longest ladder was short.

Talk about ingenious: we broke down a 20-footer,
tied one half to that 40-foot backbreaking bastard
and Marty, the smallest and craziest or bravest,
got a bucket and brush and climbed rungs single-handed.
All we could do was brace the bottom from three sides,
keep it from wanting to kick out or slide.
Talk about stupid: all for a buck fifty an hour,
no rain days, no insurance,
no one to turn to and so much to lose,
air singed with danger and no backing down.
Did we breathe while he climbed smaller and smaller
to the top? Did anyone pray til he came down?

Swear *Goddamnit, you guys*—?

At The Hyde: galleries rich
with Old Masters and Masterpieces,
Beauty's Truth and Truth's Beauty cherished for ages.
Where we stood: a world plain and simple.
This moment—and this one—or this—
as if storm clouds crackled and rumbled overhead
so we knew

this moment right here
held a lightning bolt about to blow up
the future or bless our lucky day;
three of us clenched at the foot of the ladder;
Marty's outstretched brush barely twitching—
as if he were tickling the balls of a Tawny Gold Godzilla,
all of us counting on Boy Scout knots and cheap rope,
dumb hope doing its best not to shudder or let go.

Altar Boy's First Mass

If you would imagine the nature of God,
look to what's real in this world.
                    —*Sisters of St. Joseph*

It's something like dressing out
for your first real football game.
Solemn
in full medieval armor,
deemed worthy at last:
helmet, shoulder pads, rib pads,
hip pads, thigh pads, knee pads.
You crowd doorways, overwhelm chairs.
Cleated shoes lift you above yourself.
You shuffle slick floors
wary as testing ice
to consider walking on water.
Straps, buckles, laces chafe
welts into your skin like lashes.
You worship pain's plain and simple
virtue, a gospel
of bloody noses and bruised bones.

Something like your first real date
the girl drifts in and out of
like a wish
and you a bungle of awkwardness
with no place to put your hands
or eyes
except everywhere
you've been dreaming about.

Inside, ghostly murmurings:
Come close, come close.
Let me be what you would have me be.

Original Sin

Loudspeakers hurry me to First Aid—
my five-year-old in his mother's arms.
Panic and pain pull at his eyebrows,
mouth, each an arch above an open tomb.

You know that face.
The one in Munch's *The Scream*,
hands covering ears to muffle horror.
The Vietnamese girl running naked
toward a camera, her body
immaculate a moment
before blisters and scars.

You've seen that face on all our children.
For my son, an escalator rail he didn't let go of—
or it didn't let go of him. Sobs clogging his throat,
a great breath locked inside.

When stings flash from fingers and palm
he turns over the thing gears have gnawed
to bone,
slowly raises his awful hand
as if beseeching me, or God,
or anyone who might care—
Please, may I be excused?

Coldblooded

Before Separating

You burglar bastard, you
break and enter your home
masked with just your lies showing.
Coldblooded
you, you, you, you, you.
You plan heartache, plot
to steal the rest of your life, leave
promises and victims behind.

You peckerhead professor, you
deconstruct, debate, quibble.
You nitpick nuances, you do:
"Happily Married" vs. "Happily Familied;"
"Happy" vs. "Unhappy" vs. "Not Unhappy."
Your mind is made up
of crippled memories and rotting dreams.
Buzzards haggle over your soul.

Let us pray.
Heavenly Father,
Give me strength in this hour of need.
Stop me before I don't leave again.

Selfish Wants

And so it came to pass, a Good Friday edict
from Orville Street mothers: we could forego church
this time but had to observe the Passion of the Cross
from noon to three. Quietly. Staying good
and put. No pitch and catch in the backyard. No
radios or cards or TV. No. No. No.
Just because....

If you think you can run wild just because
it's April and no school and it's nice outside
you've got another think coming and next month we'll maybe
just flush the tuition down the drain and let you all go
straight to hell and the public school with no bothers
about anything in the world but your own selfish wants.

Boys itching on the verge of teenage madness,
we'd already learned at the hands of the nuns
hopelessness once they brought God into it.
In a trance of vague devotion and knucklehead logic
we raided grocery stores outside the neighborhood
to steal Kool-Aid, candy, pretzels enough
to make it through the solemn afternoon;
mortal pleasures overpowering as the sacred
rigmarole of faith so that God still mattered but
we mattered too, something inside us not awful
but awfully changed, a bother
like the thin cut from an envelope licked wrong,
how the tongue keeps discovering itself all day.

Boss's Son

The first weeks were worst.
They were full-timers
half a generation older at least,
and me headed for college, pegged for sure
among beer drinking, beer trucking men.
And they let me know it,
their muscle cars and pick-ups more real
than jock glory and SAT's.

Whatever I'd done, they stuck
a big fat "but" on its skinny ass:
I was football captain, *but* I was quarterback—
just another name for bossing guys around.
I was strong enough, *but* I liked books.
I had a pretty girl, *but* I was pussywhipped.
My pride unraveled like a baseball's snarled insides.
So I did twice my share, blisters
torn til calluses covered my hands like shells.

Gradually, they taught me their secrets:
let your legs do the lifting and save your back.
Load last things first so pints, quarts, cans, kegs
come undone top to bottom, back to front,
first stop to last and handle everything just once.
Snugging the load, making it stay that way all day
so corners and dumbshit drivers don't tumble it away
in explosions of foam soaking up half a day's pay.

After work we hung around and drank for free.
I salvaged bottles from the cooler's breakage bin,
hosing off scum and bits of glass.
I guzzled, smoked, swore with the best of them.

Playing the boy at night, I played the man
next morning, showed up early
and tried not to puke on company time.
Paydays we went to sour-smelling hangouts
of touchy pride and easy violence. Once
I saw a logger bite off a chunk
of a guy's cheek like an apple, then promise
to wait til he got back from the emergency room.
We waited, too, and they went at it again
for what seemed a good half hour.
Blood splattered all over the alley.

Those summers I changed
into that life easy as T-shirts and steel-toed boots,
doing the grunt work and putting down salesmen
like my father with their soft hands and ties,
gloried in sweat and sore muscles and hangovers
like nobody's goddamn boss's son.
After four years I was out of college
and out of there forever. Three months later,
the artery that burst inside my father's head
dropped him to the warehouse floor and he was gone.

What did he wonder about me living so hard,
trying to prove myself to everyone but him?
It was one more thing between us
I couldn't explain and he wouldn't understand.
I wanted the world to love me, I suppose,
on its own rough terms,
but I wanted him to love me, too,
for whatever man I was or was trying to be,
for the first time not in the name of the father
but some pilgrim who could be any man's son.

Bathtub Virgin

In city and in country,
backyards and on front lawns,
dew drops bless her cheek
like tears at break of dawn.
You see her saintly splendor
grace mansions and trailer parks;
eyes of immaculate wonder
(some swear they glow at dark).

Behold the Bathtub Virgin
revered throughout the land.
If you should want one of your own,
just lend a Christian hand.
Find yourself an old bath tub;
don't chip the enamel paint.
Remove those pagan claw feet;
add a concrete Madonna saint.
Make yourself a grotto
buried upright in the ground.
Plant some plastic flowers;
dangle rosaries all around.

Consecrate your altar,
cathedral of tungsten steel.
In joys and tribulations,
bow your head and kneel.
But keep that plastic Jesus
on your dashboard whatever you do.
When Eternity waits on Judgment Day,
she'll put in a good word for you.

Umbilicus in My Daughter's Diaper

1.
Darker than blood,
black on ghostly skin,
what withered tribute
offered
to ancestral chains?

2.
Spanking new,
I learn you're mine
unequally.
Mother-linked,
Mother-loosed,
together forever
beyond
the sphere of men.

3.
Shivery serpent skin,
forsaken garden
since forgot.
And you, stranger yet—
how does the world suffer
your first
pocketful of death?

Tornado

Lake George summer day turning ugly, fast.
Temperature dropping like September.
Every dock and buoy in Paradise Bay taken.
When leading winds came on us, we were tied
to RJ's cabin cruiser for shelter, its wooden
bulk now driving us toward rocks.
All our kids below board about to be crushed
or drowned when RJ hollered,
"I can't hold her! We're going aground!"

My desperation vaulted the windshield, scrabbled
across the deck and got untied in time
for Kel to reverse the hell out of there racing
to open water, the tornado dogging us north,
RJ's cruiser lumbering behind but heavy enough
to take it. Rain pelting down, I clung to bow cleats
with both hands, spread-eagled halfway to Gull Bay.

How easy for God to make me believe again,
and I did, with any kind of prayer
left inside me. Next day, newspaper reports
of island campers crushed in tents
as winds tore down trees on their way
to do His further bidding.

I could say I took back my thanks,
flung it to the ground as a gauntlet
of defiance and compassion, howled,
Why them? Why not us? Why anybody?
But what kind of man would I be
to refuse answered prayers?
Understand: we were alive, and safe.
We were alive. We could have other days.

Sister Lard Ass

we called her, one of those squat heavy ones
you saw more of than the stalky kind
but also for the letters beginning her names
—Sister Louis Alexis or Lawrence Anne or such—
a nun's amalgamated name to prove
she came from a loving father and mother
same as us, not hatched in the convent
from a bitter black egg.

The first of three-deep blackboards would
be filled when we dumb scriveners entered
the room, and before we copied it,
up it slid and she kept on going, page after page
filling our notebooks, sentences piling up
into paragraphs multiplying
madly like loaves and fishes from hell
so on tests we could give it back word for word
for word for goodness' sake all over again,
like opposite facing mirrors in a barber shop—
images repeating themselves to themselves
into infinity and God only knows how or why.

Chemo Sabe

A while back, you said Tonto was calling
The Lone Ranger "faithful friend" when he used
the phrase "Kemo Sabe." Actually, Tonto was
calling him "he who doesn't understand" (from the
Spanish "quien no sabe"). But he was just returning
the insult. "Tonto" is Spanish for "fool."

                   –letter to editor
                   PARADE magazine

But that wasn't on my mind when your brother said,
"The next round is on me, Chemo Sabe."
Flabbergasted, I couldn't stop laughing
but it got us past the dreadful last hour
of my stupid questions and your answers
starting to make stupid sense: how the chemo
was rat-poisoning you but only partway
to save your precious Irish ass. Mean-
time, how it tore you up so bad,
every kind of food tasting like crud.
How you felt dirty all over.

When we were kids, my favorite cousins boxed
at Knights of Columbus picnics for pocket money.
Stuck in my family with three frilly sisters,
I was in awe of it all: their dazzling footwork,
their flicking jabs and vicious hooks, the beat
of leather gloves a jazzy rhythm of violence.
After the referee raised their hands in a draw,
they passed the hat and split the cash
but never spoke for the longest time.
I envied their swollen knuckles and puffy eyes.
Their silence a power that bound them forever.

So when Richard cracked us up with "Chemo Sabe,"
I thought of my cousins: how pain
creates a language of its own—or none at all.
Kemo Sabe? It means what it needs to mean.
Faithful Friend or *Masked Man* or *Fool,* or
We Who Don't Understand, or
You, You Poor Dumb Hurting Sonofabitch.
Wiseass jokes the only way
a brother tells a brother what they never say.
Outrage and outrageousness.
The dumb voice and gibberish of love.

Sister Lard Ass and the Squirt Gun

Classes were mind-numbing: copying from blackboards over-
flowing with busywork like a parable of Purgatory.
But come Spring in squirt gun season
our notebooks heavy with religious reiterations,
our cramped hands found release. Trips
to the pencil sharpener and men's room our chance
to splotch and smudge those never-ending notes

and get away with it. One day Weed got caught—
a ricochet spray, maybe, or the *squinch-squinch* of a trigger.
Then there was old Lard Ass barreling down the aisle.
She yanked the gun from his sleeve, squashed it
with her heel, slap-slap-slapped his face into a blur.
He had to sit in his seat and take it. His eyes filled
and his cheeks burned hot as her words:
"Let that be a lesson to you, Mister!"
She wheeled away, rosary beads clacking

from her hip to join those slaps still hanging in the air.
In that moment she caught the rest of us, too,
somewhere between horrified and hilarious.
But here's the lesson we remember, Mister:
two good samaritan wise guys
reaching into their desks, tossing over guns
Weed coolly emptied into his cheeks with both hands,
hurt and humiliation washed away like a caul
while we mortal sinners congregated like devils
glorious in that moment of simple grace.

Telling the Children

Our daughter the oldest, bubbliest one—
now shock quivering
in her eyes. *Separation.*
Her words
take off like frantic birds
to leave the bad news behind, delivering
us all on the wings of distraction—
the rigmarole of her day
to spare us what we don't know how to say.

When we explain *Separation....Your sister knows*
our son pulls it deep inside. His calm
measures the pain. It flows
into his fisted palms.
He stands above us. Moments stagger.
Words too plain for twisted hearts.
We rise to hold him together
as if we could start
holding together what's coming apart.

Precious ones. We love your words. Your silence.
Such eloquence
that would carry burdens so unfair
but listen: they are not yours to bear.
You are gifts from a life we shared
and offer now back to the world, pure
blessings, the everlasting best of the best we ever were.

For All You Doogey Raiders

The thing is, if you hit a guy square in the ass or shoulder
the eraser left a perfect fuzzy square, chalk outlines
marking our backs and the alley walls like

a crime scene where some body had been.
But Jumpin' Sweet Baby Jesus, what did the nuns expect?
Sending us off to detention all by ourselves, Doogey Raiders

now outcast Soldiers of Christ regrouping at 3 p.m.
and armed, by God! Our skirmishes in the alley running
between The Religious Arts Shop and O'Reilly's Irish Tavern,

even then weighing scapulars and St. Christopher's medals
against a neon juke box, men crowding the bar, laughing.
Of course we made it one more game of risk

and retaliation. What else had they drummed into our heads
from Adam and Eve and Noah into Eternity?
And something more they couldn't conceive,

desperation born of hours of busywork, answers
to be taken on faith—virtues
of submission wringing us until like water balloons

we exploded in hundreds of ways, any old brand of trouble
sweeter than the chalky taste of Catechism and confession.
Our laughter ricocheted along alley walls,

the infidel inside a wild beast
straining the long leash of heaven.
In our hands, erasers transformed into holy mischief

beating words of God into dust,
a fog like ashes drifting in the air, falling,
soon to be gone with the first hard rain.

Middle-Aged Men Just Know

"Manny's on the Run"
—carved on picnic tables
Ft. Lauderdale Beach

Middle-aged men just know
    how it goes
        their fingers edging
        rough-cut
words weathered
    smooth as their
        decent lives, double chins
        and beer bellies, all
the while out there
    Manny's on the run
        footdamnloose and fancy-
        fucking*free*
to take on every good
    badboy thing gone
        from their safely glad
        sappily ever after
sorryass middleclass
    Mr. Potato Head lives,
        the future tolerable,
        maddening
as snarls through a comb:
    that Purgatorial
        pinch and wince
        and tangle
of every-
    day ever-
        lasting
        time.

Day of the Cowboy

1.

My mother runs onto the porch in time
to see me chasing the Freihofer Bakery wagon
after the driver clucked the gray horse down the street.
I am three and already more crazy for horses than
the doughnuts and chocolate chips piled in her arms.

2.

On the backyard fence with Maureen, my six-gun
aimed at the camera's blinking eye;
later on her two-wheeler for the first time by myself,
the bike a painted pony hell-bent beneath my saddle
galloping around the block for hours.

3.

The kitchen radio Monday, Wednesday, Friday nights.
The Lone Ranger, Tonto, the Cavendish Gang
returning me to those thrilling days of yesteryear.
Heart-pounding hoofbeats, Silver and Scout
snorting and whinnying, a story that never ends.

4.

Twenty years later, my gentleman farm above the Hudson,
putting the mare up for the night. Quiet of the barn
shelter from the antiseptic stench of the VA Hospital
where my father's body hangs on for two hard years.
The stable's sweet scent of sawdust, leather, manure,
the clovered dust of hay bales shaken apart.

5.

Winter. Nightmare months tear at my sleep.
No words for those who love me,
nowhere else to go. Past midnight

combing and grooming the mare. I rub her head,
stroke the velvety muzzle. Whispers hushed
against her neck like a confessional.
She nickers, a smoky mist
that warms my hand then turns cold,
her eyes big as fists, dark as time.

I Never Heard a Nun

I never heard a nun fart
though God knows
they were beside us all our days.
Could be, holy water
kept them blessed-
ly free from vulgar expressions.
Except for June days
and Indian Summer swelter
when black wool habits hung heavy
with musky perspiration.

Sister Robert Claire was different.
She always smelled like a blend of lady
saint and real girl we could believe in.
Her tubby cheerfulness made favorites
of us barely teenage boys, made
other nuns wary and the girls jealous.

On the convent radio, she found
our Rock 'n Roll station and learned
our favorite songs. After school,
she listened
to secrets we needed to share.
Once she brought us to the gym
to teach us square dancing.
When it was time to choose partners,
we hung back from even the prettiest girls.
Each of us hoping she would take his hand.

Ex-Jock on Faith, Free Throws, Follow-Through

I believe
what the mind conceives
before the body acts
determines the aftermath.
Freeze the last motion.
Command grace with your will.
Love the flight of the ball.

I believe
the ball knows
when the body knows
what to do after
the ball is gone.
The heart's work is not done.
The ending has only begun.

Legend

Though we craved sports glory exactly the same,
at the end of high school we somehow became
cynical toward players who'd come before us
now haunting our games in a Has-Been Chorus.
Smartass and cocky, we were quick to proclaim
we'd go to college and escape fading fame.

But we questioned our fate in grown-up games
when like gospel the tale spread to awe and acclaim:
how Weed's brother got promoted rather than shamed
when the boss vetted his transcript, called him in to exclaim,
"We just checked with Siena; the college firmly disclaims
having ever enrolled any student by that name."
Weed's brother's eyes kindled sincerity's flame,
calmly inquiring, "Did you try Notre Dame?"

His Daughter Climbs a Florida Mountain

Would it be any different if it *were* a mountain
where he'd grown up? The bike old,
chipped paint, balloon tires? Truth is, it was new

as her outfit for first day in the new school.
But a flat tire and August swelter were trouble enough.
The steep turnpike overpass even more. He saw her struggling

halfway up: one hand balancing new books on the seat, the other
pushing as strangers broke around her like waves. Her face
flushed, eyes downcast ducking looks, her mind spinning—

first day… first day…worst day…worst day.
Later that week unpacking in the new house,
a commotion at the canal retaining wall.

He made like a good new neighbor,
arrived in time to see the machete arc clean
through the cottonmouth, its body thicker

than a baseball bat. For hours it writhed newly apart
from its separated head and the logic of death,
fanged jaws moving in mute greeting—

What place have you come for, my brother?
    You feel this bright new world shine
        a blessing on your old hopes? You want change
            to change you, but how will it keep you safe?

The past follows you like your sins,
your fear. Serpents come and go
in Paradise, bask in every sunlit garden.

Square Dancing with
Sister Robert Claire

First week of junior high, Kel wised off to her
same as he'd done to the one all year before.
I can still see it. Her so short, the uppercut put
all her weight under the whack of her pudgy fist
against the V of his chin. Kel arching a back-dive, landing
legs up, desks dominoing halfway up the row.
Sweet Jesus, she was tough, but bless her the first one
who liked boys best and didn't carry a grudge.

But she sure as hell wasn't one of the almost pretty nuns
you could almost imagine out there in the world.
Picture pie-faced Lou from Abbott and Costello,
lumpy-looking in any duds but now add a thick black
floor-length habit with dozens of folds, hidden pockets.
Around her waist rosary beads big as marbles
dangling to where knees would be.
Hair, ears, and neck under a stiff white wimple,
she waddled the aisles like a wooly toad.

One week she dragged us into the gym
and the alien world of square dancing—and girls.
Shedding blazers, ties, and shoes, we were cornered.
In sweat socks and knee socks, we shuffled like prisoners,
allemande left and *dosido* stranger than *dominus vobiscum*.
Robert Claire stood on a chair trying to clap rhythm
into our dumb feet, sometimes leaping down, landing
light as a blackbird. She'd skip and twirl among us
arm over arm until her habit billowed like a gown,
face aglow, God's clumsy children urged toward lessons
of possibility and romance she brought from a life before.
Reluctantly, we learned to move together, touch, let go.

First Florida Summer

(A Sequence)

The sun a doubloon from God's Bermuda shorts,
blessings you plunder and ask for more.
Mornings fresh-baked. Like honey, humidity
flavors the air. You gobble it up.

Brilliant days go black. Thunderstorms a light show
matinee every day. Sunshine comes back
shrugging its shoulders for a bright encore;
the air uncleansed, thicker than before.

Mirages shimmer from flat distances,
struggle to rise and vaporize.
You notice mountains and winding roads
. . . missing.

You miss cold days warming,
the smell of a wood fire.
You've been lying
for weeks in the same damp sheets.

Admit it. This is hell, not paradise you seek—
palm trees in cool breezes, temperate days.
Here summer is brutal, in its patient way,
but that's not what the postcards say.

Second Florida Summer

(A Sequel)

You've gone mad,
you know,
from license plates
that know you:
"The Sunshine State"
winking at you
everywhere you go—
that melanoma
they haven't yet
detected;
the state silhouette
  d r o o

        o

          p

           i

         n

          g

like the joke
you once laughed at—
Life in The Limp Dick State.
Humidity stays and stays,
soaks your breath away
no matter what
you've got to say,
licks your skin
with devilish tongues
all slobbery and prickly,
one hell of a rash
you maybe won't outlast

though you've squandered
half a drug store
on it, maybe more.

Halfway Decent Sinners

Work out your own salvation with fear and trembling.
—Saint Paul to the Philippians

"Missed mass? Skipped school?
God sees you playing Satan's fool."
                              "The clergy wrong? How dare you wonder?
                              The Vatican's spoken—'No!' in thunder."
"Mother of Mercy! Did you talk back?
Now hold still." Whack! Whack!
                              "Impure thoughts you squirm about?
                              Shush up about that. Just cast them out."

The nuns had no faith in corporal senses.
They adored Penances, Indulgences,
Catechism as dungeon, Rosaries like chains,
Hellfire, Damnation, the Holy Refrains:
Eve's sin. Adam's Fall.
Man ever wicked. God is all.
Halfway decent sinners, backs to the wall,
We held on to each other, laughing like hell.
God's honest truth? It's what saved us, that's all.

Aunt Sara

Aunt Sara's Nap

Sleep drifts away, leaves behind a groggy
tingling, this waking to him
for the first time
a surprise, like her cool nakedness,
something she maybe shouldn't trust.
She closes her eyes, murmurs,
rolls onto her side beside him.

Nuzzling her cheek upon his chest,
she molds herself around him:
her arm crosses his heart,
bending toward his neck like Cupid's bow;
she straddles his leg, warmth tight to his thigh,
breasts compressing heat at his ribs and side.

His breaths are deep, slow.
Her face rises and falls with that breathing
rocking her back into sleep
where he waits for her now, his need
greater even than their passion,
something
awfully changed and more, she knows,
than she ever dreamed of wanting.

Aunt Sara, Waiting

A softness spreading slow inside
beyond the feel of him
waits

beneath his urgency,
needing nothing but his need,
waits

as his body gusts above her
like a kite on an April day,
waits

until his sudden shuddering
stops
then she lets him slip away.

Aunt Sara and His Wedding Ring

She lays
her softnesses
along his sleeping,
his hand half a prayer
against her breast.
Slides
his ring on her finger
like the likeness of his
other woman.
Remembers
her bashlessness,
his surprise,
his eyes.
Twists
the ring,
feels
his bright malice
circling her hours,
the hurrying to sighs,
goodbyes.
Reminds
herself she barely cares,
smiles
him free, home
to his necessary life,
his sisterwife.

Aunt Sara and the Sunshower

Rain tickles the bright shoulders
of the sun splattering
tattletale rhythms
through her body's rising need,
his fingers chasing skittering
shivers bone deep.

Night overflows the afternoon,
winecool kisses on flushing skin.
As he leaves in the drying dusk,
she wonders what has ended or begun,
afraid to know, know
in these surprised sunshower days,
is he the drizzle—or the sun?

Aunt Sara's UnWedding Feast

She wants to remember everything.
How she's taken his name
to the reservation desk, now waits
alone among couples, ready to answer to
the sound of him like a magic trick
she plays on herself in a mirror.
The way candlelight romances every face.
The wine burning just enough to be fun.
How the clattering drone
settles around her like a veil.

She wants to tell him everything.
How in a way she feels married to him,
only another kind of being with him
when he's gone. Like between lovemakings
waiting for him to be back inside her, lying
beside him but floating half silly
smiling against his chest, the world turning
safe and real in bed. Afterward, how
her aloneness is real but full of him
as she takes him with her into her life.

She should tell him, she should.
The candlelight and wine, taking his name.
What she'll do is make a joke
of it, her wedding feast cooked up
with potluck passion and leftover
lust. He'll laugh, she'll watch for
the flinch in his eyes then
yes, what he does with it, how
that changes this fragile
—something—
something like love.

Aunt Sara and the Man Dying by Ounces

She weaves through chitchat, the party
a hum beyond the kitchen door.
Out on the porch, Willy hunches over a cigarette,
watches puffs rise into rain, vanish.

Black Sheep, her friend had whispered,
the family's cross to bear for thirty years, drunk
and fighting when he wasn't drying out somewhere,
trouble since he came home from the army.
For three years, dying by ounces
—a lung, half his stomach, a few feet of intestines—
nothing much left but his drinking and meanness
like now, showing up when he shouldn't,
making them ashamed for wishing he would go.

He scruffs across the porch. Each step a calculation.
The handrail wobbles, his legs stuttering him
down to the backyard. Through the window
she sees him swaying on muddy socks
nudging his shoes into a decent row.

He fumbles at his pants, takes aim.
His stream arcs through rain, splashes into his shoes.
He peels his socks, wrings them at arm's length
before he pockets them, steps into his shoes,
begins to shuffle back to the stairs.

Knowing how hope ends, she wraps his madness
in the brutal fact of dying: how
not letting go was all he had left to do,
hoarding drops as if they were minutes,
anything to slow the leaking of his days.

Aunt Sara's February Dream

She blames it on the rain.
Late winter rain a lulling sound
like waves. And all afternoon
the gray drizzle shrinking
grungy islands of snow
under eaves and ends of driveways.

The dream comes over her
like a play on their frail happiness:
a voyage with both their families
in costumes, silent at different tables.
Then shipwreck with her lover,
clinging to each other in the storm,
their bodies human, volcanic,
passion rising like landfall,
one last chance to start a new world.

The rain's pattering
tugs at her sleep. She curls into
the place where his arms would be,
tries to wrap the dream back
around her and not let go.

Aunt Sara at the Meat Counter

An aisle or two away, a baby crying.
She waits her number, looks for something
new to try, special cuts the butcher
approves with a nod. Behind him the window
doubles his smooth busyness,
his hands in no hurry but the knife
knowing its work just so, how easy
flesh opens, lets go, slides from bone.
The refrigerated bin prickles
goosebumps. Her nipples pleasure
twinging against the cold, now her blouse showing
there and there. She watches

the way she watched herself grow
to womanhood in all the windows and mirrors
of the world. Those sudden months.
The boys with their eyes on her,
and the men, too, noticing.
The crying child enters her reflection. A boy,
his face twisted with screams.
She knows she could comfort him,
her nipples warm in his mouth, how easy
to nurse any man's child, any man's.
The reflection holds her in a trance:

The butcher raises the knife to her breast.
A red trickle glides behind the blade. Blood
drops slither to her nipple and cling.
The baby in her arms, eager with small
smackings she brings to her breast
and sees in his face the face of every

lover, the knife in her hand now
against his throat
the way she always knew she would.

Aunt Sara at the Yard Sale

A harmless lark, really, just another
woman in search of salvaged treasures
she might call her own.

She parks a ways away, takes in everything
they have. A glance to be sure he's gone
but she's in no rush, an exception

to the rule of hurry up and haggle. Her ease
making love to him now a thin quiver
appraising his wife behind an apron

swollen with bills, heavy with change.
Her hands touch worn out things: coffee cups
stained and chipped, a woman's sweater

nice but not what it used to be,
bathrobes she wouldn't be caught dead
in his arms and isn't that the point? Ties

she knows as well as the scent of his neck.
Ignores picture frames, pumpkins, reindeer.
A child's revolving night light stops her:

Jack 'n Jill tumbling down the hill, circling—
a glow maybe she could read his letters by.
But it's all too much: the price of everything

or nothing and who knows what will last?
Inside, the chill begins, scrapes her bones.
She feels herself walking away

as if wobbling through riptides and waves,
feels herself going under again
with nothing new to hold onto.

Aunt Sara Forgives His 4-Letter Words

Luck
Love
Fate

Hope
Need
Wait

Vows
Duty
Harm

Can't
Must
Won't

Wife
Kids
Home

Dirty Jokes

Dirty Jokes

(for John)

If I had the wings of an angel
and the balls of a hairy baboon,
I'd fly to the top of Mt. Everest
for a heavenly pee on the moon.
—variation of schoolboy rhyme

Oh man, that's you all over, spiritual and profane,
carrying on with absurd charm. The time at the urinal
a guy blasted a fart while pissing

and you sang out, "Oh, I've seen fire and I've seen rain…
seen smelly days that I thought would never end."
The day you declared, "Scatological humor's full of crap,"

Anne and Mary vowing to bronze your tongue for posterity.
But now the cancer's back, and that's not funny.
You thought you were done 14 years ago

when they scraped out your belly, threw in some pellets,
told you not to look past a year. You survived that,
survived the divorce, the heart surgery…and now it's back

and just how much surviving can one body take?
You're serious when I call, not sure you're up to the fight
again, worried about more tumors.

In minutes it's you once more, tall tales of the operation:
"guts flailing around like spastic spaghetti,"
Keystone Kop nurses squushing your insides back inside,

bruising so bad nothing works—you're starving,
your system in trouble if it won't digest. You joke
it's back to potty patrol the way stethoscopes track

the faintest hint in your bowels like seismic rumblings;
applause for the reluctant fart, cheers for the obstinate b.m.
No shit, John, I should say, *You're such a gas,* but

I never was as quick and you beat me to the punch line
just before we hang up: "What the hell can I do?
Take it day by day, I guess....

Just keep putting... one fart in front of the other."
Hey, funny man, how'd you get so tough?
And it's true, of course. Nature's dominion

urgent and absurd far back as the womb. Vulgar expulsions—
each piss and fart and shit, each belch and slobber and vomit,
tears and ejaculations, the moon's first call for blood

to water breaking to afterbirth, the holy mess of living sent forth
from cavities of pain, sickness, love,
the body's promise we are human and dying and still carry on.

Boys Skinny-Dipping at the 'Y' in Winter

Look at us there, translucent
window blocks so thick with ice
the sun refracts a haze
of summer's golden heat.
Chlorine thickens the air
like musk, rasps our lungs.

All our bluster stripped bare.
Hands grow clumsy longing
to slouch into pockets.
Tiles resound with splashes
and hollering, hullabaloos
rising to the springboard's quickening beat—
thunk thunka: tunkety-tunk-tunk!

Water goosebumps
our skin with wicked liquidy licks,
pleasures us everywhere. Such nakedness,
how it glows, dumbstruck Eden's light
in that season of dazzled manliness.

Marrying the Lone Ranger

Soon to be newly wed
again. Still,
decades of yesteryears
haunt like reincarnations.
Her first wedding gown.
His first honeymoon.
A worry grows
sly and near as
dreams
that thrash his sleep, startle her
awake:
the wonder of all
they don't know of each other.

He knows: saying just the right
wrong thing—
how her eyes snap and
darken,
a masked stranger
and him the bad guy
he thought he'd put away for good.
His hard silences.
Stubbornness
that won't quit
no matter how he tries.
Catholic guilt clinging like sin
and no one to absolve him.
A new prayer finds him:
Make her happy.
Make this work.
Make this time last forever.

First Poem

Sister Squaw Face assigned poems
to write ourselves and read in class. Freed
from memorization and rote reply, the girls
uncovered gifts like dormant flowers. The guys
chickened out except for Kel, inspired by cousin Jake's
coconut Shrunken Head hanging in his bedroom with
bulging zombie eyes and lips laced like sneakers.
Kel marched to the front of the room,
handed her a copy, then bravely began:

The Head

> When I cannot sleep in bed,
> I get on my knees and pray to The Head.
> And when I've finally prayed to The Head,
> I find that I'm asleep in bed.

Squaw's wrinkly face re-wrinkled as if
the paper wrapped a smelly dog turd.
In the silence, Kel seemed to shrink.
Every guy in the room thanked God it wasn't him.
"You have one more to read, Mr. Kelly," Squaw said.
Kel's lip quivered as he half whispered:

The Light

> When I am afraid at night,
> I get on my knees and pray to The Light.
> And after I have prayed to The Light,
> I find that I'm asleep at night.

Well Stephen, that's a fine effort, just fine—
interesting religious subject matter
and you made them rhyme so nicely, too
is what she might have said. Instead,
Squaw sorrowfully shook her head, slowly
shredding his words into the waste basket.
The entire class rising as one, pleading together,

For God's sake, Sister, we love those poems!
is what might have happened. But we all just looked.
Kel just looked. We all said nothing.
"Take your seat, Mr. Kelly," was what she said.

Agnostic's Horoscope

PISCES: Individual you respect opens door to legitimate bargains. Focus on art objects, luxury items, patio furniture… summer holiday…. Libra figures prominently.

—Sydney Omarr
Miami Herald

Right there above Omar Sharif and Charles Goren—
where we of little faith turn first each morning. But we scorn
bridge: best-laid plans vs. luck of the draw more preposterous
than a heaven's sanctimonious saints and angel choruses.

No thank you, please. We take counsel from planetary theories,
a cosmic sense of infinite space buoyed by
galactic concern for mortal itineraries.
Today Libra arrives: friends will show me bargains to buy—

luxury items, holidays, art objects and more:
earthly pleasures a heathen's way of keeping score
like salaries and Mercedes and 2-under pars.
The heavens' oracle speaking—to me—through stars.

But now this most unsettling message to ponder:
with my whole life suddenly gone all to shit,
why do the stars in all their whirling wonder
worry about the patio furniture on which I sit?

Visiting Hours at the VA Hospital

The ambulance flashed 50 miles south
to the Medical Center, world-class surgeons and cutting edge
science poised to enter his skull. *Aneurysm* translated
by Chief of Surgery with a snap of his fingers:
"Like a small bulge in an inner tube
that one day bursts—*snap!*—justlikethat."

Weeks afterward courting recovery:
   when he first squeezed our hands;
      eyes flirting yes or no; words
         amounting to sweet nothings.
Daily rounds reported *Stable, no change.... No change.*
Slowly,   just   like   that,   our lives collapsed.
Hope.... Patience.... Outside Chance....Miracle.

... Resignation when he was shipped to the VA.
Permanent care, a language we knew by heart.
Third Class Sorryass Care where antiseptic fogs
a sour suffocation like the world's worst body odor
drenched with the world's smelliest perfume.
Green everywhere in a place without seasons.

Two years in No Man's Land, alone
in the last bed he would know.
Sheepskin pad for bedsores an inch deep.
His body retreating
into infancy: bed rails, diapers, delirious grins.
Silence deepened with every visit
as he shrank from himself, grew more like the rest,
the washed up and broken down
with gray skin, lopsided faces.
The way they looked out from their rooms like cells,

sad sack eyes begging something they couldn't say.
And others, only their backs visible in their beds,
all day staring and staring
somewhere
beyond locked windows just above their heads.

Serving Mass

Silence before mass
immaculate as Eden.
Within that silence, your joy gushes.
You are as one
with the sacred black and white
ordained by priests and nuns.
Your black cassock solemn as sin.
Surplice white with billowing grace.
Incense consecrates the one true faith;
you breathe it in like a blessing.
Your soul flows
with water and wine you pour,
takes what shape the chalice desires.
Bells you ring sing everlasting glory.

Your words sanctified with the holy tongue:
Kyrie eleison.
Christe eleison.
Gloria in excelsis Deo.
Your soul burns
with each candle you light:
the smoky stream that rising
gathers into itself your purest heart
to ascend above altar
above tabernacle
to heaven where you just know
God waits
to cherish your goodness
in the cup of His hands.

Football at Catholic School in the Undefeated Season

No more good little boy so saintly
sweet, joyfully turning the other cheek.
Your name honored with fear and praise:
Jesus he's fast!
Sumbitch is double-tough.

＿＿＿＿＿＿＿＿＿＿

No more everybody's roly-poly boy,
all those meannesses so much fun
making fun of you.
Baby Huey and *Blubber Butt*
like a miracle gone hard to muscle,
bitterness you savor like bile.

＿＿＿＿＿＿＿＿＿＿

That goose bumpy itch and twitch
before the ball is snapped—then
body brutal against body
punishing their will
until winning raises you up
like a blessing.

＿＿＿＿＿＿＿＿＿＿

A perfect season of Saturdays
glorying in deeds
worthy and everlasting:
so strong,
so full of grace,
so not yet broken.

Ruminations on Free Will
(with Pelicans)

*The great decisions of human life have... far more
to do with instincts and other mysterious unconscious
factors than with conscious will.*
–Carl Jung
Modern Man in Search of a Soul

1.
Canary yellow
the stunt kite wheels and whirls
tamed to a wicked grace.
Slithers, shimmies, skirrs.
Twin reins slacken:
it dives,
a kamikazekite
a gasp away from impassive sand,
strains against its lines
to commands of *skim*,
bank, then *soar*—
*up!*pause...*up!*pause...*up!*pause... *up!*

2.
Above . . .
on *The Yankee Clipper*,
beached tourists
hug the starboard rail,
huddle about the scuttlebutt
content to sail a grounded ship
safe from swells and spray.
Cracked lips curl around
Margaritas

and the sting of salt and tequila
helps forget shrinking skin
and unforgiving sun.

3.
Below . . .
scavengers in scruffy beards
and rope belts
troll the reeking garbage bins,
smile as they reel in
lukewarm beer and leftover wine.
They scuttle sideways,
practical as hermit crabs
lugging blanket rolls.

4.
Beyond . . .
gray against a leaden sky,
disproportionate pelicans
lumber into flight,
tumble lubberly
into a rumpled sea.

In the Year I'm Old as My Father Ever Was

What a beautiful whistler my father was.
Not the mindless type more air
than music and half under your breath,
but the complicated kind. An orchestra's
fluttering trills and deep hollows,
all of it a velvety echoing of perfection.
Mostly private, but showing off some, too.

What kind of man whistles that way?
I never met another.
And I don't remember thinking about it
back then. But now I hear it
coming from the cellar workbench,
for hours at dusk watering the lawn,
a new ghost rising from his grave
with no answers for those days
when we both had nothing to say.

My Mother, Widowed with 5 Children and Soon to Re-Marry at the Age of 49, Is Denied the Marriage Sacrament for Planning to Use Birth Control and So Confronts Her Faith

I don't care if it rains or freezes—
I am in the arms of Jesus.

I am Jesus' little lamb—
You can bet your celibate ass I am.

Her Head on His Shoulder a Wonder

He tries to understand. Her heart
thrumming his side not
at all his children's heart
except inside, that sweetest fluttering far back
when so young
them falling asleep upright against him, so far gone
from the world. Pure ex-
haustion's Zombie needing him to be there
on their way to whatever dreams.

How even then he knew how to want them to stay
that way always—
wee small Leaning Towers of Pisa and he still
keeping them safe unfalling.
He a father after years of boying it up and calling it
something better, *father* at last
at least as much as his own before and now all so long
forever always gone.

Apologies to Ma Bell

I take it back—curses I choke on when
pain-in-the-ear cellular jackasses
bray on and on.
Because today was a revelation.
A half hour fuming in traffic,
this big-haired woman in my mirror.
Truth is she was halfway homely, face
a size too small with bushy hair bursting out
high and wide like Harpo Marx
or Lassie gone wild.

Then up comes a phone she tucks under all that hair
and now she's *beaming,* lips spread over teeth just so,
eyes crinkling in the corners but not a squint,
all together *perfectly beautiful.*
The voice
of one she loves now lips brushing her forehead,
arms holding her close for as long as it takes,
a way to feel
when there's no body to touch, nothing
but words
which is all they have for now
but enough
to fill the distance between them.

The Nature of Angels and Beauty

The most important characteristic of guardian angels is not
that they are beautiful, but that they work on our behalf.
              —Angels, *Reverend Billy Graham*

In Memoriam
The reunion program lists "Married Longest," "Most Children,"
"Travelled Farthest." Ripe stuff for wisecracks:
"Most Divorced," "Most Desperate," "Most Likely to Screw,"
"Most Screwed Up," "Most Screwed Up Kids."
At the bottom of the page:
"In Memoriam: Thomas (Monk) Edwards."
So, Monk, you were first of us to go.
Just as you were first to make varsity,
your pudginess thickened to a pulling guard's
massive shoulders and thighs. In the backfield behind you,
we were slick with fake handoffs, double reverses, bootlegs.
Touchdowns and headlines came our way like pretty girls.
Your bruises like badges, and you never complained.

Mea Culpa
Hey, Monk, you traveled farther than us all!
A bad joke, wicked as the ladder jerking,
leaving you to stumble through air
and the last awful moments.
Then you were still, gone.

Benediction
Monk, Monkey Man, Ole Monker.
What bullshit they say about angels.
What word but *beautiful*
for your dirty work on our behalf?
How we swept out of the backfield

behind you, safe passage
in the wake of your nimble power,
a ferocious broad back bull,
a beautiful fist.

Cob Job

A *rough or imperfect repair.*
   —*Dictionary of American Regional English*

Piss-poor work
        and you
        you know it.
        Hammering the screw

a bit to get started.
        Cockeyed picture. Tipsy shelf.
        Wallpaper lopsided and overlap-
        ped. Facsimiles of right

angles. Screen door sprung
        —or stuck—in damp weather;
        cottonwads plug-
        ugly as mushrooms.

Extemporary, temporary, you say.
        Better than nothing.
        Close enough. Okay.
        But time will tell

on you. You know perfectly well
        the flawed things you carry
        all gnarled and sad,
        your sack of sorry excuses,

every love you ever had.

Going All the Way, First Time

Allegory—the final squawk of the chicken-hearted.
                                    —Jim Montcalm

Going all the way, first time,
is a doomed surprise like a *double entendre*—
nervous fun never again the same no matter
how many times you'll risk that metal slide
four stories high at Lake Sunnyside.
A ramp takes you where you've never been.
You vow not to turn back this time
like a sheepish child.

You sit upright on the soaped pad,
cautious for now but later you'll explore
new positions: head-first, feet-first,
belly, back, and piggyback.
You tingle so hard you're afraid you'll cry.
You take a deepest breath just before
plunging at last into the descent
that rockets you downward eyes stinging
watering so bad the world blurs by

as you fly from the end of the chute
like a skimming stone
between heaven and earth
until gravity pulls you back
to the surface of the world
and you sink, slowly,
weighed down
and buoyed by
a memory that lasts forever.

Lament of the Widow's Daughters

He ain't rich, don't live on Easy Street.
Ain't even got no puppy, got no parakeet.
And he ain't tall—5'10" in stocking feet.
A hick from mountain snow and sleet.
We don't get it, but Mom thinks he's neat:
He's got nice ears. He's got great feet.

You can see him hobbling down 17th Street.
It sure ain't pretty and it sure ain't fleet.
He's so intense and Mom's so sweet.
Will she melt like ice cream in the August heat?
We don't get it. Mom thinks he's a treat:
He's got nice ears. He's got great feet.

How will we meet him? How will we greet
When he's all tongue-tied and blushing like a beet?
They're marching to a tune with their own drumbeat.
We just caught them holding hands in the car's back seat!
We don't get it, but how can we compete?
He's got nice ears. He's got great feet.

The Widow's Reply

We're two halves alone but together we're complete.
We're two hearts together with one heartbeat.
Now Repeat.
You're two halves alone but together you're complete.
You're two hearts together with one heartbeat.

Second Marriage Polka

A gathering of clans German and Irish.
Strange rememberings—neverlasting vows long ago
when how so in love they were with others.

      Her family claps for a polka.
    A brother joins her and each cocks a leg,
      a pause to begin; then *whoosh*
    a swoop into the first step hippity-hop
     heel-and-toe and away they go
one foot chasing the other chasing the other
    gallop to glide to waltz to whirl
       perfectly together.

He watches amazed, applauds
her light footed steps so far beyond
what he can see now so perfectly
     awful—his dull shuffle through slow
             dances or worse his
    vague commotions strugg-
       ling against the beat of fast
  songs and either way her
        a tarfooted gull stuck
  with his dopey feet.

The accordion wheezes into a slow song.
She comes to him, arms open for embrace,
on her face the flaxen glow of the gloaming.

He lets go, lets himself feel
her loveliness grace his clumsy heart
like some fluky penguin astonished with flight.
When they move, they move together.
He curves into her like shadow,
she bends to him like light.

Hands Tied

The nurses blushed: "You'll have to talk to the doctor."
I stalked the halls. He walked me back
to where my father lay, wrists tied to bed rails.
"He's at himself all the time....
To keep his hands off the nurses."

The hospital hush closed over us. The end
of the lie the family'd sworn all year.
So what did that leave us with? And who?
A dirty old man with sunken eyes,
derelict's stubbled face;
infant's toothless grin from out of the fucking blue.
Where his skull was cut away, a pulse throbbing
horrible as The Creature from Outer Space.
Scenes we'd played before, he a stranger
from an alien world, I the leery bystander:

Two summers earlier when I'd taken enough crap, called out
one of "his men" in the warehouse after work, stood my ground
against the likely beating. It was me he bear-hugged to stop it,
madder and stronger than I'd ever seen, and I never knew
if inside the outraged boss was my pleased father.

And the night flashing lights woke up our street.
The whole next day he sat alone in the yard like a ghost.
Not to be bothered our mother said, telling us how
one of his men stole a truck from the warehouse.
How he had to I.D. the charred corpse best he could.
His only comment: A terrible goddamn way to die.

Years before that, a company clambake.

Full of beer and bullshit calling me over to men at the bar:
Truth, now—Think you can take your old man some day?
Something new in his eyes wanting me to say Yes.

Father, it's time to put you to rest.
All those empty visits trying to unbury the past.
The *you* that was you, gone,
and—truth, now—that was a terrible way to live.
What more would you have had me do?
Father, I loved you, I did. But was I strong enough
to have helped you go if you could have only asked?

Allegory

Before
it happens it's waiting to happen.
Two cars speeding from opposite arms
of the cross; one swerves blindly;
the other doesn't see yellow go red.
Bystanders become prophets
seeing it all slow down as if
it's already happened. Then it does.

During
the collision, senses bang and clatter.
How? and *Who's how much to blame?*
In a trance
they consider the wreck they've made,
can't remember
how they might have seen it coming.
They begin to feel
the end of ever being safe again.

Afterwards
the hub of the intersection grows
a graveyard of plastic, rubber, metal—
Island of Lost Souls swirled by breezes
from rushing cars and rumbling trucks.
Victims steer clear, know too well the signs
of old mistakes, the heart's lousy excuses.

Jesus Has Left the Building

After all these years I've been agnostic,
for my new wife's sake I go some days
(but seldom, and mercifully non-Catholic).
Current versions of The One True Word

still promising Heavenly Joys—*afterward.*
But crosses are changed from my altar boy phase
when Jesus hung exalted in exquisite pain.
Blessed wounds. Blood-drops like sanctified rain.

These versions bear no body's anguished crucifixion.
One's post is aslant, cross-arms curved into a winged dove
as if swapping The Holy Ghost for Divine Affliction.
Another's metallic; cold silhouette in a backlit alcove.
Nowhere the tormented Savior I worshipped before
I knew suffering. Mortal grace I could believe in even more.

Jim Montcalm Died for Our Sins

…in Winter storms lying our way outdoors, vows
to go straight to the Paramount for *Dr. Jekyll and Mr. Hyde,*
Invasion of the Body Snatchers. Across town,
we met at stop lights for bumper hopping,
skimming icy streets like Sasquatch water skiers
six months past summer and too stir-crazy to care.
If an angry driver got out to chase us,
the alias *Jim Montcalm*
was on our lips ready to take the blame.

…in Spring bike weather skipping school, a plot
to ride out of town and hide in the woods.
Flat broke, we talked Kel into a supply raid, nearly peed
our pants when police pulled up at the store.
Kel was fabulous: how leather jacket hoods
cornered him, swore to beat him up and take his bike
unless he stole them hot dogs and cigarettes.
The leader's name—*Jim Montcalm.*
Kel cried real hard. Later, even his mother believed it.

…the time one Summer we snuck out late;
on a dare I tight-roped the bridge railing
a hundred feet above Cooper's Cave
before cops brought us in for a long night of questions.
At dawn waiting with them on our porch, I blurted,
You know, my name's not Jim Montcalm, I'm someone else
and before they could ask *Who?* my mother charged out
crying and hitting me with both hands 'til they pulled her off.
My father's face hard, harder as the day wore on.

…all those years we embraced danger like religion
free from "Thou Shalt Not…Not…Not."

Jim Montcalm rising up to lead us safe into temptation
and deliver us from evil's painful cost.
One last chance to be saved when all seemed lost.

Agnostic and Son

As I boost him on the chair,
my students get interested—in him,
his bandaged hand, even me, teacher
turned father before their eyes.
The hand bigger than Popeye's
fist, but not funny. Under gauze
and ointment, the palm scraped
past flesh and bleeding, fingers
swollen and burst like sausages.

I go on as if he weren't there.
I could explain, but what would I say?
He's stubborn and stupid and five years old,
and the god of escalators didn't care.
But he's a good boy, trying hard
to play with the toy I let him bring.
He shifts in the chair, all his body
moving slow, the pain that rode him
through the night familiar now
in a world so awfully changed, so
wickedly strange the hand
forgets, fumbles, the wound
rubbed rough. His face tightens.
His good hand—
its name there waiting in my head—
his good hand reaches out for the bad,
cradles it, lays it down
like a precious thing. Then a deep,
filling breath, an effort to swallow
the pain. I look away, notice the girl
who turns and wipes her eyes, smudges
blotching her perfect cheeks.

Already the moment is blessed forever.
His deep breath, her quiet tears—
courage and compassion
the only sacraments I know.
The holy silence of pain,
the wordlessness of love,
the ungodly tenderness of the world.

Blue Barns Road

—in memory of my father, Gerald (Bud) Cleary, 1916-1970

1.

So I was wrong. I promised to put you to rest
but one small stop before we go.
Sound familiar? Your words
pure torture every Sunday drive, always
Just one small stop it's right on the way, five of us
stuck in the company car at the warehouse
or some bar business worth the trouble.
But it was you who also said
It's the toughest customers get the sweetest deals
and you were tough for me, Bud,
especially at the end, so let me sweeten
the lousy deal you got before I let you go.

2.

Halfway there beyond railroad tracks, the stables
on Blue Barns Road made all that waiting worthwhile:
sprawling barns royal blue, slate roofs with weather vanes,
wide open lofts flickering with swallows.
Sunshiny days, an open window and searching
for telltale blue, the luscious smell of hay and manure,
the ache of horses saddled by the road, close enough
to see inside my dreams. Bless those times

you gave in to our pestering,
just for the fun of it let yourself go
and gunned it, that slowpoke car you hated
swooping down the dip before railroad tracks
sailing over the rise with a roller coaster thrill
beyond all gravity and common sense and the shrill

screeching in our throats, that breathtaking
moment we soared magical and real
as the flying red horse on the Mobil sign—
mythical wings exalting us beyond
earth toward heavenly blue barns.

Word Farm

David Smith...spent the last two decades of his life in the
Adirondack village of Bolton Landing, working ... on the
welded sculptures that established his reputation as the
greatest American sculptor of the 20th Century. ...He placed
them outdoors in the fields near his house, where he could
study them in relation to each other and also to the trees,
the mountains, and the sky.

—Calvin Tomkin
The New Yorker

The Utica Club beer truck lugging up Tongue Mountain
from Bolton Landing on Edgecomb Pond Road.
May, summer recess, junior year of college.

This high up, morning fog lingers.
Halfway, the climb levels to a clearing—spooky
shapes shimmering in the mist.
"Deer," I say. "Damn, you think maybe a bear?"
"Nah. Tractor or hayrack or somesuch," Beech says.
"That, or given-up-on stuff from a busted truck."

Or some rough beast slouching toward Bethlehem
is what I don't say. Three years on the beer wagon
every holiday and vacation, I know how books
crowd between us, turn foolish in the cab.

None of the men at the warehouse knows
I'm engaged after going steady 7 years.
Surprise offer of her relative's diamond
and I only have to pay for the setting.

Back that first summer they busted my ass:
"Boss's Son," "College Boy."
Then it hits me: *My last summer.*
I won't be coming back

\-

My first girlfriend, beautiful
first love daring damnation
for me. The sheer thrill of lips and skin,
bodies burning up in the dark.

\-

I found out the men could be okay
when Jack helped me use the bumper,
a pad of woven rope like a ten pound pillow.
From the truck, you bounce kegs on it
to save your back and keep seams
and sidewalk from splitting. Jack said,
"Aim square in the middle just like Your Old Man's
nuts are layin' right on top," letting me know
he figured I got some ball-busting at home.

\-

Engaged. The future snuck behind me, pushing.

\-

Beech's *given-up-on stuff from a busted truck*
sings in my ear like a poem someone should write.
So maybe my head isn't completely up my ass
like so many English majors so eager to join
The Royal High Falutin' Book-Learned Club.
Or maybe I'm just scared about how smart
some of them are and never catching up.

\-

We were too Catholic for cold precautions.
Every month she bore the weight of our sins:
dread and relief flowed like forgiveness.
I'd never felt so alone or so completely loved.

\-

I hate my mother saying, "The answer's 'No.'
Because you've had enough fun for one day."

I want to take this last summer away with me.
My body strong as it will ever be. Exploring
back road short-cuts in three counties. Learning
where assholes hung out, and the best bars.
Trucker wisdom plain and timeless as haiku:

> *If you're gonna play*
> *boy at night, you gotta play*
> *man in the morning.*

> *Just because you're not*
> *happy doesn't mean you can't*
> *have a damn good time.*

> *Don't go bullshitting*
> *yourself. Saying it aint half*
> *bad don't make it good.*

On every billboard, coaster, and neon sign,
the company slogan: "U.C. for Me."

On The Freddy Freihofer Show on TV,
birthday kids got to squiggle on the Squiggle Board.
Big Jim Fisk's pen magically
made sense of the scrawl: reindeer, sailing ship, turtle.
Where's that magic pen when you need it?
Come back, Big Jim! Come back!

Once in the sacristy before serving mass,
the priest looked closely at my eye:
"Michael, do you know what a sty means?

It means you've been peeing in the road."
That surprised me because I knew I hadn't,
and there was nothing in our Catechism.
Could it be okay not to believe everything?

——————————

In Religion Study, the priest confirmed
that if mother and fetus are equally at risk
during childbirth, the Church decreed
the fetus must be saved. God had His reasons.
I swore off confession and communion
and soon church altogether.
I had my reasons.

——————————

The nuns blacked out words in our books
like unholy secrets. In back seats
and cellars we learned them all by heart.

——————————

Edgecomb Pond Road is one miserable bitch
three miles steep, narrow and winding
so you have to slow down either direction.
Hey, Beech—a great fucking metaphor
for marriage! is what I'm glad I don't say.
He's 10 years older, got three boys,
calls his wife "the old lady." He's smart
and tough. And funny. We could be friends,
but after this summer, I'm gone.

——————————

Beech has a favorite song he belts out
at red lights next to pretty girls:
Oh, I used to kiss her on the lips
but Baby, it's all over now.

——————————

Making out like crazy one night babysitting,
we answered the doorbell to a parish priest
in black fedora and heavy scarf, swaying

at the edge of porch light. Slurred words
about *counseling* or *consoling* the widow.
Apologies. We could smell his breath.

Just once, let me see a priest admit his sins;
his eyes coming out of the confessional.

Once I dreamt Jesus showed up on our porch
on Orville Street except he looked exactly like
Jack Sheehan in his cut-off sweatshirt and tool belt
that time we'd just moved in, every night my father
a dusty ghost tearing out plaster and lath.
Jack stuck out his hand: "I'm your neighbor
across the street. Show me how I can help."
He walked right in and went to work.

In Religion Study, Boo tossed me a note.
Did you hear? The new Pope
just performed his first miracle.
He made a blind man deaf.

I gave up waiting for a good laugh
from somber Bible stories, but
Sweet Suffering Jesus, grant us a sign
somewhere of a human sense of humor.

Early morning mass a chorus
of stomachs grumbling; altar boys
and priests rushed past breakfast.
Kneeling below the altar, sometimes
we'd overhear the priest let go a fart—
a gentle *poofff* or a jazzy *rat-a-tat-tat* escaping
from under his cassock. Man,
you couldn't help but giggle your ass off.
You couldn't help but like them a little more.

Beech tells me his brakes blew on a road like this
over at Hulett's Landing. For miles he ground gears
down to 1ˢᵗ, laying on the horn with his elbow
and muscling the emergency brake. An old Brockaway
with the wood-paneled cab and dashboard
so when smoke came up through floorboards,
he thought he might burn. The whole way, he says,
he could see his boys' terrified faces
in the windows of cars veering off the road.

In Religion Study, I asked, "Can God make a stone
so big He can't move it?" The priest held
that slow-burn smile as he replied,
"What is it you've been reading now, Michael?
Sure, it's the devil's thinking in you.
It's a mighty sin to turn riddles into Religion."

Say Father, ever hear about the virgin birth?
Or devouring flesh and blood and calling it holy?
What Bible have you been reading?
is what I didn't dare say.

First report Nativity Week was The Annunciation.
Mine was last: monstrous King Herod.
Did Angel Gabriel tell Mary the cost of Christmas
would be thousands of slaughtered Innocents?
Could she hear the wailing of the mothers?

My girlfriend's father, an OK guy but drinking
and wild that time, raged in her sister's room
smashing a wooden crutch everywhere.
I came running. At the headboard
her sister cringed, plaster cast to her hip.
I wrestled him down the stairs, stayed

to make sure he didn't come back.
Her parents never once mentioned it—
me a Knight in Shining Armor
shivering in underpants.

I wanted to save them from that life.
I wanted to beat him 'til he cringed.

Jake, Kel, and me at urinals in the Boys' Room.
Satellite Sam, custodian with a lump on his forehead
the size of a golf ball, mopped the stalls behind us.
As we zipped up to go, he hollered, "You little bastards!
You go get the hell out of here!" his mop whapping our backs
as we played 3 Stooges jammed in the doorway
then stampeding down the hall. We were innocent
that time, but who'd believe us? And it *was* hilarious,
so we offered it up to Purgatory, ransom for dozens
of sins undetected—fire-crackered toilets, peeled oranges
splattering the ceiling. God moves in mysterious ways,
we knew, so maybe Sam was sent to do God's bidding.

That whole summer I halfway know
I'm pushing her away, a vague worry
shaping me in mean ways. I burrow into work's
uncomplicated sameness: mapped-out routes
north-south/east-west with no turning back
on yourself. Organizing cans, bottles, kegs
first stop to last; free beer from the cooler after
kicking the ass of another tough day.

Six months later I've lost her.
Too many broken dates; too many
small cruel things. The next year,
the week she's to marry, I see them
in a new Mustang convertible. Hunter green.

She laughs as she touches his cheek.

_____

Half a year after that, my father will go down
on the warehouse floor and be gone forever
though he wastes away in a VA bed for 2 years.
Sometimes his eyes seem happy as a baby's.
I'm sorry and *Goodbye* is what I never get to say.

_____

I should've said *I'm sorry* to her a hundred times
though it wouldn't have changed *Goodbye*.
I was afraid to let go of something gone,
some precious habit or dumb hope—
like the sign I saw on a copy machine:
"Do Not Use. Almost Broken."

_____

Fog's burned off as we head down the mountain.
We look for whatever was hidden in the field.
No deer, no trucks. Bizarre angles and curves—
scrap metal, bronze, stainless steel welded into
abstractions: humongous what-nots, alien creatures
and iron beasts sixty or seventy strong
commanding the earth like nothing seen before.
In the out-building, a man in heavy gloves
with tongs and hammer works red-hot metal
in the glow of a forge. I think of an old-time monk.

_____

Next semester in Art History, I'll discover
Picasso's *Bull's Head*— nothing but an ordinary
bicycle seat, handlebars, and his vision
leaping straight into my mind forever.
Later, slides of David Smith's "Sculpture Farm"
take me back to that field that day:
what seemed A Mad Hatter's Parade
of Old Mistakes and Leftover Things
like hearts after they tear each other,

are torn, then touched by grace
and made whole again.

Those rusty shapes and shining figures
were my first glimpse of beauty
reflecting the breathtaking
common world I lived in. Scraps
of junk and nearly forgotten things
forged by hammer and fire
toward earthly resurrection:
unlikely gods and beautiful monsters
rising like sparks showering
lost Eden's long night's air.

Afterword

Reader's Revenge Sonnet

[Select the choice which best matches your response.]

1.___I can't stand poems that don't even rhyme.
   ___Same sounds are a bore and a snore all the time.

2.___Not serious enough; too frivolous and silly.
   ___Too grim: sin and death give me the willys.

3.___The short ones are best—you can stop and think.
   ___Too abrupt—gone with a blink.

4.___The ones I could follow took their time and were long.
   ___If too much is said, something's wrong.

5.___All that talk about God, nuns, and priests.
   ___He's finding his way. He's still trying, at least.

6.___The language is awful—*ass*, *fuck*, and *turd*.
   ___If you can't say what's real, why write a word?

7.___Those people he speaks of—what will they say!
   ___I guess they're just human; they sounded that way.

[Add additional comments as necessary.
All refunds redeemed in heaven.]

Notes

"Lucky Shirt": *Sisyphus'* punishment for revealing the gods' secrets was to push a large rock up a steep hill, only to exhaust his strength and see it roll back down every day. His story has been seen as a comment on the absurdity of earthly life in the shadow of death as well as a tribute to the human spirit in the face of endless suffering.

"Paramount Theater: Solipsism in the '50s": *Solipsism*: the theory that one's self is the only thing that truly can be known and verified.

"Learning Picasso": From John Keats' "Ode on a Grecian Urn:" "Beauty is truth, truth beauty—that is all/Ye need to know on earth, and all ye need to know." The Hyde Collection in Glens Falls, NY, houses numerous renowned art works such as Rubens' *Head of a Negro*, Rembrandt's *Portrait of Christ*, Picasso's *Boy Holding a Blue Vase*, Degas' *Dancer with Red Stockings*, Renoir's *Coco*, Homer's *A Good One, Adirondacks*.

"Bathtub Virgin": Suggested in correspondence with Fred Sullivan, tough left tackle, Doogey Raider, and Adirondack film-maker. Rest in peace, Boom-Boom.

"Chemo Sabe": For Kel and Richard; John and Terry.

"Football at Catholic School in the Undefeated Season": For St. Mary's Academy's undefeated Northern Conference Champions, 1961-62. A shortage of teaching nuns led to the closing of the high school several years later.

"Ruminations on Free Will (with Pelicans)": The Yankee Clipper Hotel on Ft. Lauderdale Beach is shaped like a cruise ship.

"Word Farm": Italicized line in 3rd stanza from "The Second Coming," by William Butler Yeats.

Michael Cleary is a former altar boy and graduate of St. Mary's Academy in Glens Falls, NY. Residing in Ft. Lauderdale, Florida, since 1978, he has published essays on authors such as Flannery O'Connor, Harold Pinter, Edward Albee, Thomas Berger; his poems appear widely in journals and anthologies. He is a two-time recipient of a Florida Arts Grant in Poetry, Featured Lecturer for the National Endowment for the Humanities, winner of the 2005 Paumanok Visiting Writers Award, and recipient of an Endowed Teaching Chair at Broward Community College. His collection of poems, *Hometown, USA*, won San Diego Poets Press' 1992 American Book Series Award.